Buttons, Doodahs and Wotnots

A Young Poet's View of Today's World

by Francesca Thorscott

Published by JJ Moffs Independent Book Publisher 2023

JJ Moffs Independent Book Publisher Ltd
Bawtry Hall, South Parade, Bawtry, Doncaster DN10 6JH

ISBN 9781739191627

Typesetting and cover design by Anna Richards www.design-by-anna.co.uk
Illustrations by Sadie McGlone

Contents

The Fall 1
The Forever Train 2
Forest Dogs 4
Cat's Eyes 5
Tracker and Attacker 6
The Feather 8
Staring Eye 11
Man of the Ocean and Widow of the Wind 12
On the Old and Rickety Railway Track 14
The Ice Castle 16
The Miniatures 18
There I Was 19
A Perilous Journey 20
The Fungi Forest 22
Kahhukamoroe 24
A Gull's View 26
The Junkyard on the Top of Our House 28
Lockdown 30
Scoundrel's Theft 32
The Ladybird 33
Rainbow 34
Wartime Words 36
Shadow 38
Wartime Blast 39
Remembrance Day 40
The Spirit in the Crowd 41
The Great Wood Dragon of Dralus 42
Did You Know? 43
'Twas the Plight Before Christmas 44
Spider 46
The Queen 47
Sweet Dried Raspberries 48
The Pebble in the Lake 49
What I Am 50
What I Do 51
Imagining 52
Words of Wisdom 54

Introduction

Francesca began writing from a very young age and developed her love of poetry through reading rhyming stories. The poems in her book "Buttons, Doodahs and Wotnots" begin with ones written at just eight years of age through to being twelve years old. Her aptitude for seeing things differently from her peers has always been apparent and she is not afraid to stand up and be individual.

Her poetry talent was first noticed when she began writing frequently at that earlier stage. She would have a picture to use as a reference point or be verbally given a subject to write about. Her words flowed from the pen and she found it effortless to write her poems, whether they were short or long. Her Scoundrel's Theft poem received encouraging and positive comments from David Walliams with special consideration to the language used. Her passionate writing about the planet gained a beautiful and personal reply from Sir David Attenborough.

Many adults in the world of teaching and writing have given positive reviews of Francesca's work and she hopes to inspire other young people to pick up a pen and write how they feel or to convey how they see the world around them.

The Fall

Forgetting her worries and her woes,
Gripping on tight with fingers and toes.
Leaving behind her anger and strife
Risking her passion, her limb and her life.
As it's up to the heavens she goes, she goes
It's up to the heavens she goes.

Such a brave traveller, eager and clever
Will she stop climbing? Oh, will she? Never!
Ascending forever for the rest of her years
Leaving her family, colleagues and peers.
As it's into the skies she goes, she goes.
It's into the skies she goes.

As the world drops far below
She starts to dizzy herself, you know.
Gazing at her scale of height
It towers above the ground, such a fright!
Now it's tumbling down she goes, she goes.
It's tumbling down she goes.

As she descends she catches a rung.
As she got her grip, how tightly she clung!
Gaining her grasp and resuming her rise
Getting back to where she made an accidental dive.
So it's above the clouds she goes, she goes
It's high above the clouds she goes...

The Forever Train

Leaves are cluttering up the floor,
A train passes by, but with no door.
For that train runs on those tracks
And its passengers, they don't look back.
For everything is always the same
Running on the forever train.

Through an ever long tunnel they soon pass,
Yes, that's impossible, I thought you'd ask.
And on their trip they did see
A pirate ship, a bright red tree.
For nothing normal is ever the same
When you're on the forever train.

A pink and yellow starling high in the sky.
A tree whose branches spelled out "why"?
The passengers, they had some rye
Before munching on waffles and apple pie.
Nothing ever makes any sense
The nonsense level of my poem's immense!

They see a blackbird, swoop and glide,
A giant tsunami, nearing the tide,
A floating cake, a war of peace,
A cow, which had a yellow fleece.
You can't complain, it's never the same,
Sitting in the forever train.

Forest Dogs

There are six dogs who live in a tree.
They come out and they play with me.
It is I who built their houses, green
In the tree trunks, tall and lean.
It is I who built their houses, green
In the tree trunks, tall and lean.

They are called Bertie, Chocolate and Max
Biscuits, Monty and then there's Bax.
And they all scavenge for food in the forest
And they do really well, if I'm honest.
And they all scavenge for food in the forest
And they do really well, if I'm honest.

We all help them travel along their way.
And remember, they are a pack, not strays.
But really they are quite civilised.
And stay away from hunters' eyes.
But really they are quite civilised.
And stay away from hunters' eyes.

Cat's Eyes

A little black cat that stares at you
His little black eyes, promising and true.
His pretty little whiskers fine and sleek,
A stare so fresh but pale and bleak.

His nose, he twitches it about
And waves it in the air like a long snout.
And now those eyes, they stare at the moon
All shiny, like a silver doubloon.

Then they move on to this big black man
What's he holding? A spoon? Some keys, a fan?
The cat, whose eyes were now used to the darkness
Spied on the robber with their night time sharpness.

So the cat got ready to pounce
And did so with a hint of flounce.
He bounced straight off a lamppost
And landed on the thieving host.

People arrived to see
What had happened under the willow tree.
The cat was held up before
Everyone; he was a stray no more.

Tracker and Attacker

Lapping up the cool liquid,
There lay a majestic beast.
Resting on the chalky rock,
Preparing for a feast.
Ready to pounce upon his prey
Silent and unseen.
All set to leap into the air
And tumble into the deep ravine.

Yet over in the grasslands stood,
A mighty competitor, strong and good.
Deviously observing the unwary tracker,
Cunningly plotting to be a good-souled attacker.

Both malicious animals planning their move.
Both convinced they will have victory.
One false move and they'll be finished;
Their rival is fierce; it could be the end of their story.
Suddenly, the tracker turns
Seeing the attacker, his eyes burn.
Tis because he detests his opponent with passion,
So for him, he really had no compassion.

The pair of beasts, they ripped and tore.
Until their tongues and teeth were sore.
But when the horrid fight was over
All temper was gone and peace won over.

The Feather

In a clearing in the forest,
Sat a lady, true and honest.
With her black frock
And violet locks
And eyes of emerald green.
Her slender body, tall and lean.

In the distance, those eyes spied,
Across the land, far and wide.
A gleaming feather in its down
All shiny and pearly, like a crown.
Glistening in the morning sun
Enough light to blind everyone.

Racing towards her, strong and bright,
No-one withstanding the feather's might.
Floating on the breath of day,
Flying like a jackdaw or jay.
Approaching the lady, ever faster
Flying so fast it could end in disaster!

Now the feather put on the brakes,
And (clumsily) almost landed in the lakes!
Descending much more slowly now
And nearly landed on a cow!
Floating down into her palm,
Her heart stopped thumping: she became calm.

Her feet they rose up off the floor
The cow rose up off all fours.
She looked down at the forest to say bye
As the feather took her high, high, high.
Soon the land below was blurred
As she was carried away from her human herd.

The feather slowly declined in its pace.
It seemed to realise the journey wasn't a race.
Treating the lady as if she was its daughter
Now falling, but floating as if in water.
Softly it landed in a shrine
In the middle of the Land of Shine.

The houses were encrusted with gold and gems.
Topped with gold domes sprouting silver stems.
On top of diamond stilts there sat
A grand palace, whereat
The king and queen greeted the lass
And said "We shall have tea with this underclass".

The tea was lavish, plentiful and feastly.
And tasted the complete opposite of beastly.
Roast turkey, caviar, lobster and wine
The finest wine you could call fine.
They ate and drank with gay abandon
Much more than you and I ever have done!

When (at last) it was time to leave,
The king and queen let the lady receive
Golden gifts from the Land of Shine
To put at home, in her own shrine.
Now the feather swept her away again.
Back home to the forest in the glen.

As the lady was swept home
She sang a little happy poem.
'Home again, home again,
Swishing around in the air again.
Home again, home again,
Back to my home in the glade again'.

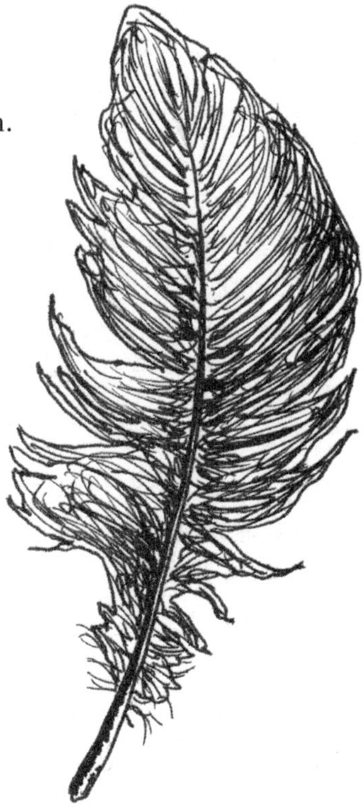

In the forest dark and gloomy,
With the night noises eerie, scary.
Sat the lady with the feather, worn.
In the black frock now weathered and torn.
Waiting for the sun to once more rise,
Waiting for an adventure surprise.

Now she goes on adventures constantly
And takes hold of the feather confidently.
Visiting land after land after land
The Land of Water, the Land of Sand.
Now she dreams with eyes wide open
All hope of living normal life was broken.

So if you're in the forest one day
And a shiny feather flies your way.
You know what to do,
It awaits you.
Catch hold the feather and fly away
Visit a new land every day...

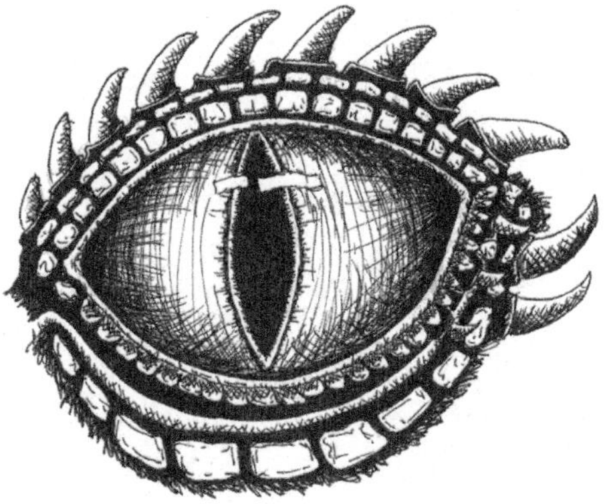

Staring Eye

Lurking in the depths of the murky woodland,
Alert to a twig snap in the muddy sand,
Staying still so not to arouse suspicion,
There lay camouflaged like an apparition,
Spread out like a log lay a dangerous beast
Snout long and thin, belly screaming for a feast.
The eye is a deep green, like the swirling sea,
Waves crashing like evil itching to be free.
A yellow dust, like pollen from a flower,
Sprinkles the eye, like an old ancient power.
The pupil is a slit, like a black plant shoot,
The surrounding skin is as tough as a boot.
A sniff of the air and a twitch of its hide,
An unfortunate creature, as prey, it's spied.
There are thousands of ferrets in the woods, no doubt,
Like there is in rivers, haddock or trout.
At the sight of food the beast produced a smirk
Teeming with teeth, razor sharp, as a dirk!
Beasts are terrible, no doubt about that.
They come very different, scaly or fat.
They are scattered across the range of the globe,
Some known, like Nessie, or the one in the robes.
All beasts and monsters have one thing in common,
All can be hidden from the closed minds of humans.

Man of the Ocean and Widow of the Wind

Waves are swishing, bashing, colliding
And the tides are silently rising.
The Man of the Ocean is controlling the shore
Elusive be he, the man of folklore.
Recalling the water to turn it away
Your shallow waters you play in day by day.

He is but a myth, this man in my tale,
Who curls up by the rocks near the shore to wail.
He sides with the Widow of the Wind to make peace
And to make the fights of water and wind cease.
The pair go out together every day
To play with the children when they come out to play.

The children so quickly run out to the beach
To try and make a sandcastle each.
The man slowed the tide and the widow made a breeze
Then cleared clouds from the sun so they wouldn't freeze.
When the children at last finished their play
The man reached out and washed the castles away.

The man and the widow swept all castles away
So the children could play another day.
The Man of the Ocean went back to the sea
The Widow of the Wind followed he.
Today and for many years to come
They will make beaches fun for everyone.

On the Old and Rickety Railway Track

Over the rocks and ferny wood,
Over the hill where the old tree stood.
Over the lakes and high up terrain
Through the sun, the storm and the rain.
And through the gaps twigs go snap! bang! crack!
On the old and rickety railway track.

Over the ocean that glistens and shines
Down through the rocky ruby mines,
Up past the valley the deer and the cattle
Scatter as the track it does rattle.
We see bulls are fighting, bash! bosh! smack!
On the old and rickety railway track.

Through the tunnels carved by the moles
Up and down, from north to south poles.
North to south and east to west
Everyone knows our vehicle's golden crest.
Being famous it does not lack
On the old and rickety railway track.

Soon the sky darkens to deep blue
There are nocturnal animals: snow foxes, snow shrews.
The great lights sprout from the sky
And it is up to those lights we fly.
We see oranges, greens, red, blue and black
On the old and rickety railway track.

DANGER!
MINES!

The Ice Castle

Animals freeze, cautious and wary
Skin lies on the ice, once soft and hairy.
But now, bodies rotting and bones ready to snap
The skulls of trespassers who fell in the trap.
Statues of those who tried to break the wall,
But alas, those statues aren't statues at all.

The walls of the castle are covered in ice.
A huge snow ramp designed not to entice.
With spiky stone spires that could cut through steel
And a beautiful porch the shape of a wheel.
Icicles loiter like long silver thread
Just the sight of the spike fills any creature with dread.

Penguins turn away and point down their beaks
When, from nearby the castle, there comes a shriek.
A wail so eerie, high and shrill
It could extract the soul from a brave man at will.
The sky starts to pour and the ice mountains crumble.
The temperature drops and the ground, it does rumble.

The shriek comes from a woman who is old and frail.
Her clothes are tatty and her skin is pale.
She died of the cold here centuries ago
Now so does everyone - friend or foe.
She built the castle, mountains and the icicles sharp
And now she listens to her magic ice harp.

The Miniatures

When the house was empty and all was quiet,
They filled up the sink and began a riot,
By adding bubbles to the water, oh bubbles galore!
Overflowing the sink, it drips onto the floor.
Using the tap like a diving board,
And the tooth picks as big rubber swords.

The overflow and a hole in the wall for a slide
Two paper clips to help get in from the side.
Dolls' house seats and toilet paper towels
Ear cleaner woggles look like long dowels.
With tablet beach balls and polo rubber rings
Oh what joy, the lack of humans brings!

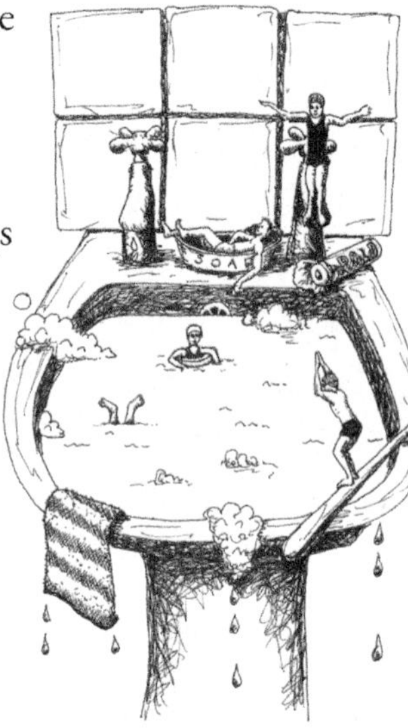

Tooth floss swings like rope they hang
Cotton snaps with an epic twang.
Across to the toilet for the children like to
Flush and make music, and to me and you
They are so tiny they're a pin prick, all pink.
Those miniatures living under our sink.

There I Was

There I was, alone,
Sat on cold wet stone,
Just waiting for her
To turn up, occur,
But she never will.
The mist, murky, still,
The lanterns so bright
All say that she might.
Stunning red flowers,
Like mystical powers,
They do tease me so
For I do not know
If they're enough
For me to gain love.
And, all through the night,
I thought that it might.
When the mist does clear
It shows a lady, dear
Shadowed you should know
As the sun rays show
Behind my love.
At the song of the dove,
My fingers crossed tight
I hope that she might...

A Perilous Journey

Alone I stride.
Far down the rocky mountainside
Wending my way down an icy path
No steaming dinner, or fiery hearth
To comfort me.
The street lamps flicker endlessly
And, though of rest, I have gained none.
I've no food or water, but I must go on.

The click, click, clack
Of my cane on the freezing track
And scraping paws of the polar bear
With its cream fur coat so thick, so fair
So wild and free.
Yet, I am bound so helplessly.
Snow dusted trees are watching one.
They are all watching me, but I have to go on.

The gale picks up,
Hurling round a new born pup.
Penguins shiver and ruffle their coats.
Unworldly lands unharmed by boats
To break the ice.
I clutch my precious parcel tight.
Delivery time, parcel sent, hooray!
But now I must get back, yet another journey.

The Fungi Forest

Down in the marshes where fungi do dwell,
Live many creatures whose tales we do tell.
Tales told so badly they're hard to believe
When they're near us, it's we they deceive,
And though people otherwise might protest,
It does exist, the fungi forest.

In the middle of the lake there is a door
On the murky bottom of the deep lake floor,
And if you stepped through the door you would find
A fantastic sight which baffles the mind.
Everything mushroom - the houses and rest.
That's what it's like, the fungi forest.

Down from a house hangs a fraying long rope,
Lowering a pot and a dog, with a hope.
Ten thousand fungi with stalks tall as trees
The sun and a storm and a drifting light breeze.
Houses with weather vanes and broken carts,
Small glowing lights to guide tiny hearts.

I was once told of a land of mushrooms
With no lingering smog or dirty fumes.
Clearer clean waters and brighter blue skies,
Tastier pastries and fresh apple pies.
Where there's no richest and there's no poorest,
For I was once told of the fungi forest.

Kahhukamoroe

Kahhukamoroe,
Where wonders go,
Things getting so obscure
That no mortal could ever endure.

Danger for danger,
Things getting stranger,
The vision is surreal.
Tropics in water so cold you can't feel.

Monsters and mermaids
Wreaths made of flow'r braids,
Buildings not rotted down.
Weird and eerie - the mysterious town.

The deluge seeping
and women's weeping
Into every scope.
The scale of destruction doesn't leave much hope.

Whispers are fading,
Stories cascading
To places forgotten.
Tied up in chains and out with tight cotton.

High buildings crumble,
Topple and tumble
To the doom down below.
What happens next you might not want to know…

A Gull's View

The frothy, white wave advancing closer,
Grumbling, groaning, ready to enclose her.
Him and him, going to swallow them all,
The large, crushing wave, twenty metres tall.
They might be excited, worried as well
But I am neither; it's safe where I dwell.
I fly up and up again up near the clouds
I'm not down with the unsafe growing crowds.
The salt and the spray is covering their faces.
Wind and wave are racing their paces.
Excited murmurs, frightened wails and screams
People think they're all having bad dreams.
The dirty seawater and the crashing waves
Anticipation, like tigers behave,
Wild and free like the gathering wall
Standing over a hundred metres tall.
I'm the gull soaring over the ocean,
Watching these happenings motion by motion.
The events that happened from build to fall
The wall that stood a hundred metres tall.

The Junkyard on the Top of Our House

Whenever you feel the need to grouse,
Just pay a short visit to our house.
We'll take all your worries and throw them away,
By showing you an old wooden stairway.
A ladder of oak wood, so polished and bright,
When you see what's above your heart will take flight.
A mess of old rubbish that nobody needs;
Old Lego pieces and extension leads,
Boxes and boxes of Christmassy items,
Lovely souvenir German Zeitungen.
You might see a spider and a play list by Strauss,
When you're in the junkyard on the top of our house.
Millions of cobwebs and a small woodlouse,
Lie in the junkyard on top of our house.
A gold darts award and a young lady's coat,
A bunch of old guns, could've shot a stoat!
Hundreds and hundreds of children's stuffed toys,
And a musical doll that gave many joys.
Thousands of books of a child, less than seven,
An unticking clock from a house down in Devon,
Encased in a box and dumped into the dust,
String that would disintegrate in a strong gust.
It's really an attic, but quiet as a mouse,
I call it the junkyard on top of our house!

1st
Odd Socks
LEGO
5+

Lockdown

On the local A road no traffic sits
Because everyone is on lockdown.
The only people about are the twits
Because everyone is on lockdown.
A deserted London, so eerie
Because everyone is on lockdown.
If you enter the shops, no-one will you see
Because everyone is on lockdown.
All on a virtual shopping trip
Because everyone is on lockdown.
No-one at the pool taking a dip
Because everyone is on lockdown.
Just, for once, the weather is fine
Because everyone is on lockdown.
You can't smell the fumes, just the damp, wet pine
Because everyone is on lockdown.
DIY stores have gone right out of stock
Because everyone is on lockdown.
Planting daffodils and blue hollyhocks
Because everyone is on lockdown.
Seeing family, just through a window
Because everyone is on lockdown.
Using media to see all who we know
Because everyone is on lockdown.
Smoke and gas clear for the first time in years
Because everyone is on lockdown.

Ending the lockdown, to my eyes, brings tears
Because I shall much miss this lockdown.
It's the break this world needed so very much
YOU helped the planet… brilliant lockdown.
Though it is sad to know why that we are
On this fabulous, helpful, great lockdown
We must remember it's for our good after all
That everyone is on lockdown.
As the atmosphere is thriving more
Because everyone is on lockdown.
Our eco system was dead on the floor
But now everyone is on lockdown
Less trees are burnt, toppled or chopped down
Because everyone is on lockdown.
Please stay hygienic, stay eco-right now
Because the world should stay on this lockdown.

Scoundrel's Theft

Scurry, scurry, fur-clothen thief,
Thou warpéd, toad-spotted vassal,
Eth harlot the acorns to grief,
Caused thine farmers great hassle.

Therehence, thou clapper-clawed creature
A light-fingered thief, that is thee,
Kill you even will the preacher
A promise to you, a decree.

To be, or not to be your fate,
Thine demon, he darkens thy soul,
These actions thou's life shall debate,
Afore in death thee enrol.

Thy farmer shall do deeds uncouth,
He chaseth, followed by love's glee,
He has his son, still of youth,
And fair maidens, his daughters three.

Thou weedy, unchin-snouted miscreant,
Who harlot thy acorn? No gent!
To thee, black curses have been sent,
Thou foul, dismal-dreaming rodent!

The Ladybird

I am adorned, decorated with red,
But surrounded by more stunning beauty.
The ne'er ending dark has its own glory
I'm not pretty, compared to it, you see.
Upon which I stand is a white feather,
A swirling, luminescent bird's wing
On a sky-blue, reflecting, glistening lake,
Compared to them, I'm an ugly red thing.
I look at the clear, yet misty water,
And try to see my small self as the best,
Like an heiress, so grand and almighty,
Forget the small me that is honest.
But all I can see is the grandest,
The towering Phoenix of sun's son; flame
The imposing bird that if wrong is done
Makes you feel as though you are one to blame.
But in the Phoenix's eyes, a new picture,
A new version of life and creation,
One that shows me as the great, grand Phoenix,
And my heart skips in joy and elation.
Now, past the luminescent feather, gone,
And the thought of the sun setting off west.
The lake, Phoenix, mountains all creation,
Does not sadden me; I'm me, I'm the best.

Rainbow

Red is for the sweet flowers,
The poppies and the roses,
The colour of the man's cheeks
When he, at last, proposes.
Also symbolises rage,
The chill on the cold winter noses.

Orange for the fiery flame,
For the sweet scent of itself.
The cosy, cinnamon smell,
And beneath the mantle shelf.
The tang of the sweet citrus,
Lining for intricate delph.

Yellow is a joyful mix
Of happiness and sunshine.
Spring, the sun and buttercups,
When bathed in yellow; divine.
Tennis balls, fluorescent coats,
A flame to in romance dine.

Green, when light is a freshness,
When dark, is mellow as earth.
The grass, plants, leaves and some frogs
Are coloured like this at birth.
In things from eyes to bottles
A colour of great, great worth.

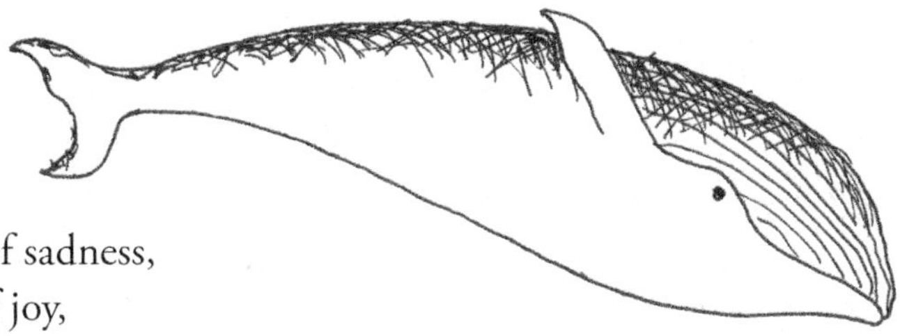

Blue; a colour of sadness,
Also a colour of joy,
Symbolising the bright sky,
The oceans and seas; land Ahoy!
Night skies with constellations,
Rivers, fish, whales, carp and koi.

Indigo – pastille purple,
But thought of as purple pink,
Pretty and bright, happy, light,
A wonderful colour, I think.
But it's popularity,
Needs to be brought from the brink.

Violet – the last colour,
A purpley, blue shade is,
Beautifully mellow and,
Found with the Wildman with his
Wild blueberries growing free.
Through the rainbow we have
whizzed.

Ah! The rainbow! At last! Here!
The rainbow! The rainbow! Hark!
Hip hooray! Hip hip hooray!
Our world shall never be dark.
We've this colourful array!
The sun and rain! Party! Lark!

The Rainbow! The Rainbow! The Rainbow!

Wartime Words

War, the armies, navy, air force,
No time for regret or remorse.
The bullets, shot, causing death and pain,
Killing for England's right to reign.
Shocking loss on the battlefield
In trenches the wounded concealed,
'til the nurses can heal from afar,
To be living, how lucky they are.
The trenches, cold and damp, like night
With bustling men, close sounds of fight.
With only some tea and a letter,
Some sit, thinking of times far better.
Out on the waves, more fighting men
Aim to shoot or sink their brethren.
The mariners, the naval folk
Trying desperately to war revoke.
However, in the smoggy clouds
Where it rains not but misty fog shrouds.
Mighty machines patrol through the sky
Shooting and dropping bombs as they fly.
Spitfires, Tornadoes, Hurricanes
The bombers, the murdering planes,
Destroying the wall so neatly laid
Guarding to try and stop an air raid.
But they didn't always succeed
Keeping England of gasses freed.
Sirens wailed and homes were vacated;
Things got far too far from placated.
Wars, undoubtedly full of death,
And many a foeman's last breath.
But, at last, when the fighting does cease,
There remains not a war, but a peace.

Shadow

Shadow, oh shadow,
You do follow me
Wherever I go
Or do I follow you?
Please tell me, who is to know?
You'll be there for me
I'll be there for you
And if I can't see
You; the sun it does hide
You're there, for a team are we.
In front, round the back
To the left, to the right
You never do slack
Just show all my movements
The moment dawn it does crack.
Shoulders to cry on
When I am so sad.
A source to rely on
When times are hard going.
For some, a bed to lie on.
Shadow, oh shadow
You don't follow me
Wherever I go
Because I follow you
That I do know.

Wartime Blast

They were awake and they had time to sprint,
Away through the barren landscape of flint,
Through the mud, dead trees, and old metal scraps
That form on this waste land nothing but traps.
Through pools of water only dead men once drank.
Past an old sink hole where a whole troop sank.
If only they turned in panic they'd see
Two young men called up too; Willy and me.
We ran from the hide out, an old stone cave,
We yelled as loud as we could, we ran and waved,
But see or hear us alas they did not.
Tired and drained our run slowed down to a trot.
Pure fear drove us on, the bomb would explode,
The wood would ignite, close to our abode.
Aha! Our comrades! They climb in a pit!
Only a shame that we made it… as grit.

Remembrance Day

We stand here; in disgrace,
On top of the place,
That cost many young men their lives.
From the dusk to the dawn,
Cause many to mourn;
Their parents, their children, their wives.
But all that I can do,
Is stand just like you,
And know that my roots in the ground
Grow from those in the earth,
Who died without mirth,
And no hands to hold to be found.
Our few petals are red,
Like blood of men dead,
Our seeds are the sorrow they cause.
Our leaves face eleven,
For when on heaven,
The world take a silent pause.
We're not really concealed,
In Flanders great field,
We'd rather be picked at the stem.
At eleven each year,
There, there, there and here,
We will always remember them.

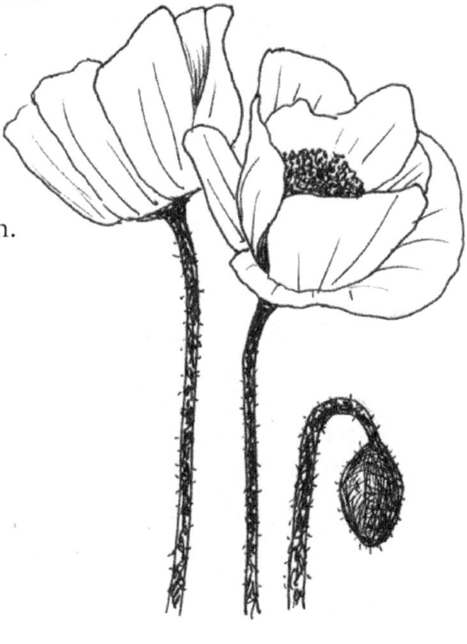

The Spirit in the Crowd

Frightened and alone on the bustling streets,
The sea of black umbrellas stretches far,
Heavy drops of water my scarlet shield meets,
The sky and people blend in with the tar.
Shoving and pushing is the only way on,
So people too polite won't get around.
If something is dropped, then it's as good as gone,
For you could bet your life it won't be found.
Then, oh so suddenly, from out of nowhere,
A tangled mass of limbs drenched to the bone,
Speeding through the crowds neither hither nor there,
Taking flight to most others quite unknown.
The soaking mass of limbs is gone from my sight,
Except for fleeting glimpses through the crowd,
I run with determination and great might
But never find the spirit in the crowd.

The Great Wood Dragon of Dralus

Long, long ago in ancient times, the wizard Dralin was born,
He took many shapes, from angry bulls to low and humble fauns,
He became King of Dralus and ever since he was crowned,
The wood dragon of Dralus atop the palace is found.
His wings, like a bat's, so sleek and so fine,
Ready to beat at the Army's front line.
His teeth sharp as knives, his eyes... how they stare,
His claws so strong, through steel they could tear.
Placing his claws so steadily and firm,
His fiery breath so ready to burn,
Smoulder and scorch and set all ablaze
Leaving no evil to cough in the haze.
Yet the Dragon of Dralus isn't so tame,
His promise to save all granted him fame.
He comes to the aid of all who mean well,
And those untrustworthy he shall expel.

Did You Know?

Did you know that grass is blue?
That the sky is pink and green?
Did you know that I'm a gnu
And you are a runner bean?
Did you know that wood's a tease?
It's quite false and misleading.
In fact, it's not at all from trees
It's made by Emperor Ming.
Did you know that ice is hot
And bananas come from bees?
Did you know that rain is snot
And if you get warm you'll freeze?
Did you know that frogs are sad
Because of purple Mondays?
Did you know that good is bad
And bakers bake on Bundays?
Did you know that up is down?
Did you know that left is right?
Did you know a cloud is brown?
Did you know that bingbongs fight?
All of this is very real
To all of you at home
So with one last burst, I'll seal
This truthful, truthful poem.
All of this is very wrong
Although I've said it's not.
This poem's very, very long.
And did you know I've stopped?

'Twas the Plight Before Christmas

'Twas the night before Christmas,
And all through the house,
Ev'ry creature was stirring
Even a mouse.
The children were waking,
Alert in their beds,
Whilst dreams of winged sugar plums
Left their sweet heads.
Mama abandoned her kerchief,
And I took off my cap,
Knowing our unsettled brains
Would get no winter's nap.
For out on the lawn,
There rose such a clatter.
Somebody shouted,
And something did shatter.
Away to the window,
I flew like a flash,
Tore open the shutter
And drew up the sash...
The moon on the crest
Of the new fallen snow
Gave the lustre of midday
To objects below.
When what to my wandering
Eyes should appear,
But a crash-landed sleigh,
And eight tangled reindeer!

With their old rotund driver,
His head in the snow
His trousers a'ripping,
And his buttocks on show.
Less rapid than snails
The coursers they came
So Santa struggled and shouted
And called them by name:
"Oh Dasher, oh Dancer,
Oh Prancer and Vixen,
Help, Comet! Help, Cupid!
Help, Donner and Blitzen!"
So the reindeer all heaved
And pulled St. Nick free
His head popped from the snow,
He could finally see!
He saw us all staring
From the window inside
So climbed back on his sleigh
(Many times, he tried.)
But I heard him exclaim
'ere he drove out of sight:
"MCBC* to all
And to all a goodnight."

**Merry Chuffin' Blummin' Christmas!!! - this came from one year when this was exclaimed as everything was going wrong in the house around Christmas!*

Spider

Perhaps it wouldn't be so bad
If you didn't have eight legs.
But then, you use them, I suppose,
When you are climbing walls, like pegs.
Perhaps it wouldn't be so bad
If you didn't have a presence.
Sometimes you make the air so thick
You'd make a fortune off the essence.
Perhaps it wouldn't be so bad
If you weren't so frightfully fast.
Race a human and some spiders
And your human will finish last.
Perhaps it wouldn't be so bad
If you simply were not there.
All you do is eat flies and frogs do that
So, yes, I think that's fair.

The Queen

A constant in a time of new
A friendly face to me and you
And now to Heaven, God has beckoned
Our monarch, Queen Elizabeth the second.

Cloaked in sadness you shall perceive
Our shocked and shaken country grieve
For now the world shall hear us sing
God save her son, Charles, the King.

Sweet Dried Raspberries

I'm hungry now. What do I do?
Tea is at four and it's only two.
I'm starving, and I need to eat
I don't want bread, cheese, eggs or meat.
Oh no! A tragedy! A shame!
I'll have to eat chocolate again.
But that won't help. I need something crunchy
Something healthy, good for munching.
A tub of something pink and bright
Full of sweet and tart delight.
The answer comes to me with ease
I'll have some sweet, dried raspberries!
They're bitter, dry and very nice
I'll have a couple, then some ice.
I'll have one, two, three, maybe four
Oops! Dropped that one on the floor.
I'll have to have one to make up
Then maybe a Chupa Chup.
Nah. These raspberries are far too good.
I wonder if I really should.
Have eaten – what, ten, fifteen pieces?
Then, at last, my hunger ceases.
I sit back down. It's quarter past.
I certainly ate those fast.
Just one more – NO! Show control
Soon you'll have your bacon roll.
Yeah but that's two hours away.
NO! Save them for another day.

The Pebble in the Lake

On a boat, a gentle rock
To the rhythm of a clock
Port and starboard, left and right
In the woody mountain lake at night.

A swinging arm, a false try
The pebble in the palm is smooth and dry.
The momentum gains, the pebble leaves the hand
It sings to the lake, one note as it lands.

The circles reach the sandy edge
And the jutting outcrop of the rocky ledge.
The lake is filled with a silent song.
The water stretches ripples long.

The pebble sinks, the murky gloom
Engulfs the pebble in its doom
To sit and wait and wait some more
On the dark and chilling lake bed floor.

What I Am

I am the silence in the clamour
I am the dull amongst the glamour.
I am the stillness in the raging sea,
I am nothing, I am me.

I am the light in the pitch black dark.
I am the smoothness of age withered bark.
I am the colour in the old TV
I am nowhere, I am me.

I am the one who shuts weary eyes.
I am the stars beyond the skies.
I am here, you just don't see.
I am everywhere, I am me.

What I Do

I laugh, I cry,
I work and play,
These are the things
I do by day.

I sleep, I dream,
Turn out the light,
These are the things
I do by night.

I see a world
Of good and bad
Then I see you
And I am glad.

I study hard
I try so much.
I bring my pain
To your healing touch.

I wake, I eat,
I lay, I walk,
I sit and stand
I jump and talk.

I look, I frown
I shout, I blink.
I look at you
Then grin and wink.

I hear, I smell,
I taste, I see
I touch, I feel
I am, I be.

Imagining

This job that I'm doing? It's boring.
And then I've got homework too.
But if I don't get all my homework done
Future Me has no job to pursue.

I'd rather be on a pirate ship,
Or flying above the stars,
Or in a forest, the sea, or a volcano,
Or putting bad people behind bars.

I've thought about it too much now.
There is nothing that can be done.
There's adventure, a mystery, danger,
A battle to be lost and won.

Buttons, doodahs and wotnots
Are pressed in the bridge of my brain
I'm sorry but it isn't my fault
If I'm off imagining again.

I feel in the back of my conscience
A familiar tug at my soul
Like myself, my mind, the me bit,
Has fallen down a bottomless hole.

A villain, a hero
A king, a queen
What will be, what is
And all that has been.

Wait, what? Is that somebody speaking?
Do they want me to make a choice?
I must find something fitting to say
And reply in a confident voice.

Then with a crash I'm snapped back to reality,
A world without magical things
Like enchantresses, fairies and dragons,
Pirates or magical rings.

Words of Wisdom

Those who wander are not lost,
So wander together no matter the cost.
Money is a futile thing,
So be with the ones that money can't bring.
Better by far to be hungry and cold,
Than in cosy warmth with no hand to hold.

Printed in Great Britain
by Amazon

20957506R00038